My Senses and How They Work

My Senses and How They Work

Written by
Marie Cortissoz

Illustrated by
Sally Springer

kidsbooks
Incorporated

Copyright © 1994 Kidsbooks, Inc.
3535 West Peterson Avenue
Chicago, IL 60659

ISBN: 1-56156-316-1

Manufactured in the United States of America

Contents

Introduction

When I go to the zoo with a friend, we sometimes play a game. I close my eyes and she leads me while I try to guess what's all around us.

First my friend leads me to a fence. We stand very quietly and listen for sounds. I hear a loud "Rooooaaaar" and I know we're standing in front of the lion's cage.

Next my friend pushes my hand onto something warm and furry. I hear a soft "baa" and I know I'm petting a lamb.

Then we take a break and sit on a bench that feels hard and scratchy. It must be wood.

Soon I begin to smell something good. What is that smell? Maybe it's butter?

"Open your mouth," my friend says. In pops something salty and chewy.

I open my eyes and look around. I see the popcorn my friend is holding. I see animals and trees and people smiling at us.

When I told my teacher about our game, she said I was using my senses to learn about our world. My five senses let me **see, hear, smell, taste,** and **feel.** Maybe you have some questions about how your senses work? I know I do!

Sight and Seeing

Have you ever wondered why it is hard to see in the dark?

That's because your eyes need light to see. 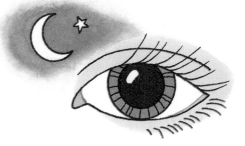 During the day, light bounces off of everything around you. The light hits water and you see a pond. The light hits a person and you recognize a friend.

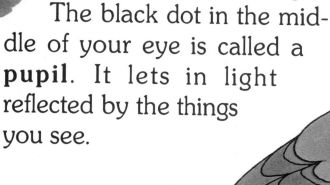

The black dot in the middle of your eye is called a **pupil**. It lets in light reflected by the things you see.

Light goes through the pupil and passes through a **lens**. The lens directs light to the back lining of the eyeball, called the **retina,** where it forms an image. Like a movie screen, the retina plays pictures of the things you look at.

Images on your retina are all upside down. These upside-down pictures travel to your **brain** along a pathway called the **optic nerve**. It is your brain that knows how to turn the pictures right side up. You need both your eyes and your brain to see.

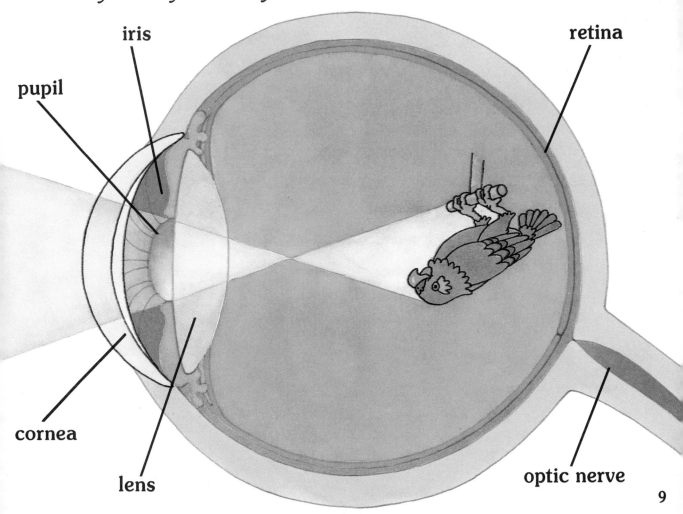

iris

retina

pupil

cornea

lens

optic nerve

How do you see in the dark?

When it is completely dark, you can't see anything at all. But often when it seems very dark, there is really enough light from the moon or the stars or a nearby lamp for you to see. When it is dark, your pupil widens to let as much light as possible into your eye.

Why do I have two eyes?

You have two eyes so you can see more. Each of your eyes sees a slightly different picture. Stare straight ahead and close one eye. What is the farthest thing you can see on both sides of you? Now open your other eye and look from side to side. Do you see more?

What are my eyelashes and eyebrows for?

Your eyelashes and eyebrows help keep things out of your eyes. Your eyebrows also help keep the sun out of your eyes when it is shining over you.

Why do I blink?

Sometimes you blink to protect your eyes. If someone throws a ball at you when you're not looking, your eyelids quickly close to try to keep your eyes safe. Most of  the time, you blink because your eyes need to be kept wet. Blinking spreads your tears around and keeps your eyes healthy. A blink lasts for about one-third of a second. You blink thousands of times a day.

Why do some people wear glasses?

Many people do not see well. When they look at something across a street or even across a room, it may be blurry. Some people can see things clearly that are far away, but the words on a book right in front of them may be fuzzy.

How do glasses work?

People who do not see well usually have problems with the lenses in their eyes. Their lenses do not direct light correctly. They don't project images onto the retina. What people see then, seems blurry. But the lenses in a pair of glasses help the eyes direct light, putting images on the retina where they should be. Then a person can see clearly.

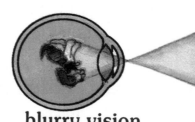

blurry vision

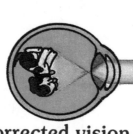

corrected vision

eyeglass lens

Sound and Hearing

Your ears let you hear many things. When a colt whinnies, a baby cries, or a friend plays a guitar, you hear sound. Sound is made when something moves so fast that it **vibrates**.

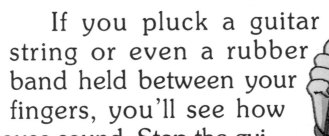

cock-a-doodle-doo O

If you pluck a guitar string or even a rubber band held between your fingers, you'll see how motion can cause sound. Stop the guitar string from moving and the sound will also stop. If you press your hand against your neck while you are talking you will feel how voice muscles vibrate.

Vibrations travel through the air to your ears. The part of your ear that you can see, called the **outer ear**, captures sound and funnels it through a tube to the **eardrum**. The eardrum is tightly covered by a layer of skin. When hit by sound, the eardrum begins to vibrate. That vibration moves three tiny bones in the **middle ear**. The movement of those bones strengthens the sounds you hear.

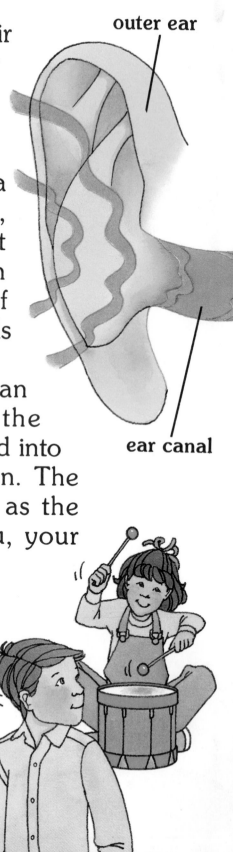

outer ear

ear canal

The vibrations then move to an inner portion of the ear called the **cochlea**. There, sounds are changed into messages that are sent to the brain. The brain recognizes those messages as the sound of your mother calling you, your friend laughing, or a siren wailing.

Why do I need two ears?

Having two ears helps you figure out where a sound is coming from. When you hear a strange sound, you may move your head without thinking

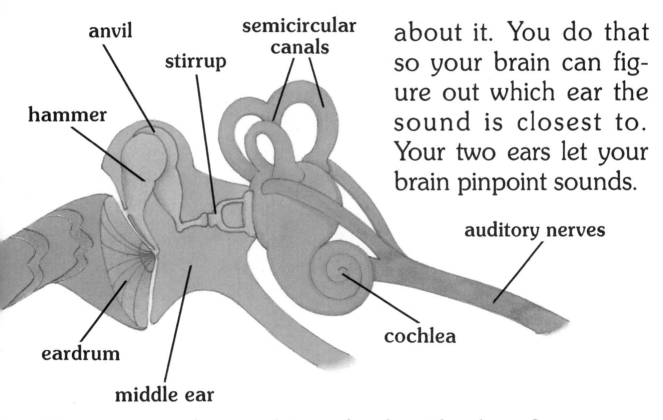

anvil

semicircular canals

stirrup

hammer

auditory nerves

eardrum

cochlea

middle ear

about it. You do that so your brain can figure out which ear the sound is closest to. Your two ears let your brain pinpoint sounds.

Do my ears do anything else besides hear?

It may seem strange, but your ears help you dance, hop, and run. Next to the cochlea are three small tubes filled with liquid. These tubes help you keep your balance by sending signals to your brain. When you twirl around, the liquid shakes and your brain knows you're spinning. But if you stop suddenly, you may fall over or feel dizzy because your brain will think you're still moving, until the liquid stops!

Why do I have wax in my ears?

The **ear canal** is filled with a sticky, orange-brown wax that protects your ears from dirt and dust. The wax catches dirt that enters the ear and pushes it out.

Why do my ears "pop" when I ride in an elevator or an airplane?

Air is always pressing on both sides of your eardrum. As you get further off the ground, the air is thinner and doesn't press as hard as the air in your middle ear. When you swallow, you bring some of the thinner air into your ear. Then your ear will feel the same pressure on both sides.

Why can some people wiggle their ears?

Rabbits, deer, and many other animals move their ears to follow sounds. They hear better when their ears face the direction of a sound. A long, long time ago, people may have also been able to move their ears around. Some people today can still wiggle their ears a little. But that doesn't let them hear any better!

Smell and Smelling

Does your nose ever tell you that dinner is cooking? Does it let you know the grass has been mowed? Does it warn you that the milk has been around too long?

When you want to smell a rose, you sniff it. That sniff draws air deep into your nose. When tiny bits of the flower,

olfactory nerve

nasal openings

nerve endings

called **molecules**, reach the upper part of your nose, they waken special detectors called **olfactory nerves**. Those detectors carry messages about the smell or odor to the brain. It is your brain that knows it is sniffing a rose.

Tiny bits of food, perfume, spoiled milk, and anything else that gives off an odor also mix with the air you breathe. Those odor molecules are too small for you to see. You can smell them only after they mix with water. Luckily, the lining of your nose stays moist enough to do that job.

Some things release more bits of odors when they are heated or broken. That is why you can smell hamburgers better when they are grilling or grass better after it has been cut.

Why can't I smell things when I have a cold?

You can't breathe well through your nose when you have a cold because its lining swells up the way your ankle would if you hurt it. If an odor can't reach the olfactory nerves located high up in the nose, you won't be able to smell.

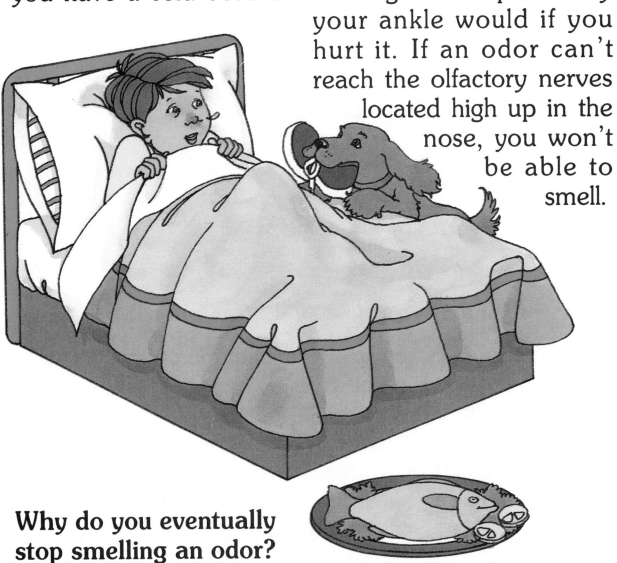

Why do you eventually stop smelling an odor?

Your nose becomes tired if it keeps smelling the same odor. Once you get used to an odor, such as the perfume you're wearing or the fish cooked for dinner, your brain no longer notices it.

How important is the sense of smell?

Unlike some animals, you don't need your sense of smell to find food or notice enemies. But your nose can warn you not to eat food that is spoiled. It can also prepare your body to eat. Just think how much you enjoy taking deep breaths in a bakery!

Do we smell in the same way that animals do?

Many animals can smell things that are very far away from them. Dogs can find their owners or someone who is lost by trailing their scent. Dogs can even sniff out food that is buried in the ground. Although people need to be closer to objects in order to smell them, people can smell a larger variety of odors than many animals can.

Taste and Tasting

What part of your body do you think you use to taste your food? If you guessed your tongue, you're on the right track! But your tongue also gets help from your nose.

If you look at a friend's tongue, you'll see it is covered with many little bumps. Inside those bumps are **taste buds** that recognize four different tastes: sweet, salty, bitter, and sour. The taste buds for sweet foods are on the front of your tongue. Bitter foods are tasted on the back of your tongue. And you taste salty and sour foods on the sides of your tongue.

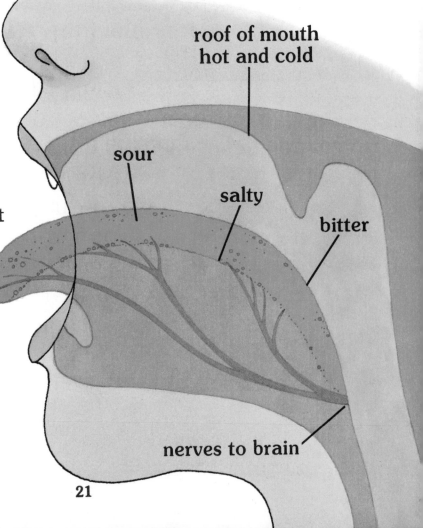

roof of mouth
hot and cold

sour

salty

bitter

sweet

nerves to brain

When particles of food mix with the watery **saliva** in your mouth, your taste buds recognize one or more of the four flavors and send messages to your brain.

Your tongue can taste the sweet sugar in both strawberry and chocolate ice cream. But you can tell the difference between the two flavors because they have different smells. When you eat something, its smell is carried up your throat to your nose. You enjoy a food's flavor after the brain hears from both the tongue and the nose.

1. Get two different flavored ice-cream cones.

3. See if you can tell which ice-cream cone you are eating. Then let go of your nose and try again.

2. Close your eyes and hold your nose.

How many taste buds do I have?

You have about 10,000 taste buds. Most of your taste buds are on your tongue. There are also a few in your throat and on the roof of your mouth.

Do my taste buds always taste in the same way?

Your taste buds work best when food isn't too hot or too cold. That's why a bowl of soup has more flavor when it cools down and why ice cream tastes better when it melts a little.

Why does food taste differently when I have a cold?

When your nose is stuffed up, you do not smell your food. You cannot enjoy the full taste of a food when your brain is just getting messages from your tongue. That's why a lot of food tastes the same when you're sick.

Does my tongue do anything else besides taste food?

Your tongue also helps you talk. It must move for you to make certain sounds. Can you say "lollipop" without moving your tongue? How about "mother?"

Touch and Touching

How do you know that a kitten is soft and a rock is hard? Why do you get goose-bumps when you jump into cold water? How can you tell if you've scraped your knee?

Your skin sends messages to your brain all day long. Through your skin, you feel. You have thousands of **nerves** scattered throughout your skin. Some nerves feel cold or heat. Others feel pain. Still others respond to the hard pressure of a push or the light touch of a butterfly landing on you.

3 feet

25

Under your skin, nerve endings wrap around the hairs on your body. That is why you know if someone lightly touches your hair. Your skin uses the nerves to send information to your brain.

You reach out to feel things with your fingertips because they have more nerves for touching than any other part of your body.

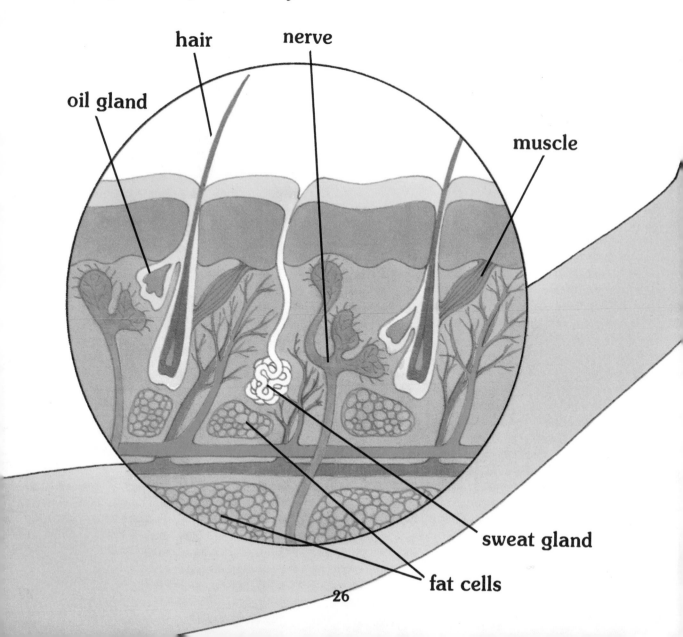

hair

nerve

oil gland

muscle

sweat gland

fat cells

Why does the body need to feel pain?

Pain is one of the ways your body protects you. If you touch a hot pan by accident, you immediately pull away. Your nerves warn your brain of the danger and in a flash your brain tells your hand to move.

Why do I feel pain when I am sick?

Pain helps alert you to an illness or injury. If a pain is bad enough, you know you need to see a doctor. Pain also makes you rest when your body needs to heal. You won't run if your leg hurts or stuff yourself with candy if your stomach aches.

Why does chilly water stop feeling cold after I've been swimming for awhile?

Your body can get used to many different feelings. After a while, your brain will stop paying attention to certain messages if they stay the same. Your body doesn't usually get used to pain, however, because that would turn off its warning system.

Does my skin have other jobs besides touching?

Your skin helps keep many germs that cause illness out of your body. It helps protect your heart, lungs, and other organs from injury and the sun. It also keeps your body's temperature from changing wildly when it is very hot or very cold outside.

Glossary

Brain: The body's control center. The brain collects messages sent from other parts of the body, then tells the body how to respond.

Cochlea: The snail-shaped part of the inner ear. It receives sound vibrations from the middle ear, then sends these messages to the brain.

Eardrum: Located at the entrance to the middle ear, the eardrum vibrates when hit by sound, then sends the vibrations to the cochlea.

Ear canal: A one-inch long tube that runs from the outer ear to the eardrum. The part of the canal nearest the outside produces wax to help trap dirt.

Lens: The part of the eye that focuses light rays, just like the lens of a camera.

Middle ear: A small cavity that carries sound waves from the eardrum to the inner ear through a chain of tiny bones called the hammer, the anvil, and the stirrup.

Molecule: The smallest part of something still having the characteristics of that thing. A molecule is so small it cannot be seen by the eye.

Nerves: The paths through which messages travel between the brain and other parts of the body. For example, when your hand touches a hot stove, nerves send a message of pain to your brain, which then tells your hand to pull away!

Olfactory nerve: The nerve of smell. It sends messages from the nose to the brain.

Optic nerve: The nerve of sight. It sends images from the retina of the eye to the brain.

Pupil: The hole in the middle of the eye that looks like a black dot. The pupil narrows and widens to control the amount of light coming into the eye. It gets larger in the dark and smaller in bright sunlight.

Retina: Located on the back lining of the eyeball, the retina receives images from the lens. But the images on the retina are upside down! So the retina sends the images to the brain, via the optic nerve, where they are turned right side up.

Saliva: A watery fluid in the mouth. Saliva keeps the mouth moist and helps dissolve food so it can be tasted. It also helps the body begin digesting food.

Taste buds: These help the body taste. Found on the tongue, taste buds tell the body whether a food is salty, bitter, sour, or sweet.

Vibrate: To move quickly back and forth when touched or hit by sound. For example, a guitar string vibrates when strummed.